TO: *Linda*

FROM: *Mom Anderson*

We cherish the hearts of those we love,
for it is around those hearts that our
lives revolve.

Heartstrings

Fay Angus

illustrated by Peter Church

The C. R. Gibson Company
Norwalk, CT 06856

Love is the melody of the soul
that keeps our hearts singing!

It is love, glorious love, that sets
us right side up in a topsy-turvey
world. . . .

Like the kiss of the morning sun, love
is the light that brightens up our
darkness, puts rainbows on our path
and brings us the comfort of heart's ease at
day's end.

For love to thrive and grow, love must
court love and tickle it in all the
right places.

Love with laughter is love with luster.

We need to write ourselves a daily note:

Take time to laugh together.
Take time to dance a little jig.
Take time to celebrate each other.

Love is an investment—it should pay
regular dividends.

Fun is the luster in love. It puts
breathing space into our day-to-day
relationships, lifts us out of the
doldrums of a humdrum routine and
lightens up our hearts.

Love and laughter. . .

Joybells of the heart.

Big dreams dreamed, grandiose plans
planned and a destiny to be shared
stimulate love, but small simple
things also brighten the eyes of love.

A picnic at the beach to loll about
and listen to the sound of the surf;
run hand-in-hand, and heart-to-heart,
barefoot along the sand...a friendly
chase ending with a tease and tickle
to flop exhausted and watch the clouds
hurl animal shapes across the sky.

The smug delight of a well-kept secret...
a hide-away, just you and me ...an interlude of
love romanced morning, noon and
night.

Love is time invested in each other.

SPACES in our love
keep us reaching for
each other.

Spaces are gifts that say. . .

*Thanks for letting
me be me.*

Love squints when it looks only into the eyes of its beloved. We become emotionally crosseyed if we look only to each other for fulfillment of happiness. It is a wise saying, "Love is not merely looking into each other's eyes, but looking out together in the same direction."

Time alone makes time together more pleasurable.

We can celebrate our differences. . .

When we can encourage each other to
develop our God-given talents,
individual interests and pursuits. . .

then we can snuggle in
to talk about them.

Like the tide, love joins and then
separates from the shores of our
souls. . .constant and unchanging.

God gave us arms to wrap around each other.

A loving touch and tender stroke soothes our spirit and salves our wounds. From the time that we are born, we have a yearning to be touched and held . . . that yearning never leaves us.

And the ecstasy of a boisterous hug that squeezes the very breath from us . . . and twirls us round about . . . is love's lively jamboree.

God gave us eyes to be the mirror image
of our secret self.

Enchanting, captivating eyes, all reflecting pools
of love-light.

God gave us ears to listen to the well-springs of
each other's hearts.

*The ear is the gateway to
the heart.*

Love not only listens—love hears. . .
the undertones as well as the overtones. . .
quivering silences that sometimes speak
more loudly than our words.

I will stitch a banner to fly above
my home. It will say. . .

LOVE SPOKEN HERE

Tell me that you love me. . .yes, yes,
please count the ways.

Sing and shout and whisper all the
endearments that catch the heartstrings
of our love and twine them together
like the long ribbons and bright bow
in a spring bouquet.

Loving words have the power to make the
plain beautiful, the poor rich, and bring
new life and hope to those who despair.

A love story for the ages. . .

"I love you beyond breath, beyond reason, beyond love's own power of loving. Your name is like a golden bell hung in my heart, and when I think of you I tremble and the bell swings and rings!"

Cyrano de Bergerac

We love each other not only for what
we are, but for what we become when
we are together.

Tucked into my night stand drawer is
a copy of a love note, written by an
unknown author whom I would love to know...

"I love you for putting your hand into
my heaped-up heart, and passing over all
the foolish, frivolous and weak things
which you cannot help but dimly see there,
and, instead, drawing out into the light
all the beautiful, radiant possibilities
in me that no one else had looked quite
far enough to find!

I love you for closing your eyes to the
discords in me and for laying firm hold
of the good in me. . .

I love you because you are helping me
to make of the lumber of my life not
a tavern but a Temple, and of the words
of my every day, not a reproach but a
song. . . ."

The measure of love is love without measure.

Love is unconditional. It gives and gives and gives. . .and then it gives some more.

To make rules for love would be to dilute it. Love is love—it is not dependent on the if/and/or/but of its performance.

Love stands alone enshrined in the
splendor of its own merit. The joy
of love is caught in the dimensions of
its multi-hued style.

*Different strokes for different
folks, all blended together
to add color and texture to the
relationships in our lives.*

Love is not blind to flaws, but
kindles tender mercies around those
flaws. Love puts its focus on what
we are, rather than on what we are not.

Love has a syncopated beat . . . a mutual give and take.

Love is a verb . . . it actively participates.

The building blocks of love. . .

courtesy

caring

kindness

commitment. . .

The gift of a **caring** heart is the sweetest gift of love.

Turgenev, the great Russian novelist, said that he would give all his fame and fortune for someone who cared whether or not he came home at night.

Courtesy is the grace of love. **Kindness** is its touchstone.

In everything we do and say, do kindly, in the kindest way.

Commitment is the working force. It works to work things out.

Commitment takes as its directive. . .

Never let a problem to be solved become more important than a person to be loved.

Love forgives.

Oh, the bumbles of our bitter pride
that snuff our joy, when all the
while our hearts are longing to
forgive. . . to be forgiven. . . to love. . .
to be loved!

Reconciliation knits us to the heart
of God.

"Love that reaches up is adoration.

Love that reaches out is affection.

Love that reaches down is compassion.

Love that stoops is grace."

Love reaches for its greatest joy when it learns to dance with the wind of Heaven!

The love of God spills over so that it nourishes all other love and puts a harmony between our love and the love of those who love us.

The love of God is the "joy of heaven to earth come down."

*The love of God is the tuning fork that
sets the pitch for the melody of love.*

The love of God is thoughtful, considerate,
patient and kind.

The love of God does not keep score.
It forgives without hesitation or limit.

God's love is totally accepting and
unconditional. He loves us for who
we are, not because of what we do.

When we learn to love as God loves, we
love with a love beyond ourselves, a
love that reaches for eternity.